Meditation

The Transformative Impacts Of Meditation On One's Existence A Comprehensive Analysis Of Meditation's Profound Impact On Contemporary Society

(How To Attain Wellness And Contentment Through Enhanced Self-Awareness)

Pantaleo Rossini

TABLE OF CONTENT

Seeking The Earthly Kingdom To Be Transformed 1

The Principles And Rationale Underlying The Practice Of Meditation 13

Advantages Of Meditation Practice 26

Practicing Mindfulness Meditation 59

Traditional And Integrative Methods For Promoting Wellness 73

Why Start Today? 95

Strategies For Expediting The Process Of Falling Asleep 102

A Brief Five-Minute Meditation For Relaxation Post-Work 121

Seeking The Earthly Kingdom To Be Transformed

This leads us to the subsequent issue, predicament, potential, or extraordinary possibility associated with unlocking the key at the subsequent stage. "As it is in heaven, so should it be on earth" (Matthew 6:10, King James Version). Jesus declared to Peter, upon bestowing upon him a new name, that he would be entrusted with the authority of the kingdom, stating, "I grant you the authority to bind on earth whatever shall also be bound in heaven, and to loosen on earth whatever shall also be loosened in heaven" (Matthew 16:19 KJV). The transformation of our earthly desires into desires of a celestial nature is imperative. Our hearts and minds must undergo a transformation, shifting our focus from worldly desires to those of a celestial nature. The heart/mind contributes to the process of metamorphosis. According to the book of Proverbs, chapter 4, verse 23, it is advised to exercise caution and mindfulness in one's thoughts, as they possess the power to shape one's life (GNT translation). In an alternative rendition, the verse reads as follows: 'Guard your heart diligently, for it is the source from which life's outcomes flow' (Proverbs 4:23, King James Version). This represents the pivotal moment of transformation within the prayer." "This marks the fundamental turning point in the prayer." "This denotes the crucial phase of metamorphosis in the prayer. The essence of transition lies in our comprehension of the imperative for the conversion of this antiquated realm into a fresh one, the metamorphosis of our former disposition into a novel one, soiled appendages into immaculate ones, and the purification of impure hearts into virtuous ones.

With divine assistance, we have the ability to undertake a proactive approach in bringing about a metamorphosis both internally and externally. We develop a comprehensive understanding of the entities and ideologies that we are engaged in combat with. Paul, in his message found in the book of Ephesians (6:12), articulates that our struggles are not with mere human beings, but with entities of higher authority such as principalities, powers, rulers immersed in the darkness of this world, and manifestations of spiritual malevolence present in high positions. This insight was captured in the King James Version for reference.

It is imperative that we partake in virtuousness and embrace God's unwavering love unceasingly. We recognize the imperative for the embodiment of celestial virtues, primarily love, in our earthly realm. We aspire for our actions on this planet to mirror the virtuous demeanor witnessed in heaven, characterized by profound love and the act of granting forgiveness. Our motives become clear. The unwavering love bestowed upon us by God aids in fostering trust in His guidance, especially in times when fear attempts to influence our choices. Love empowers us to foster reconciliation amidst the challenges posed by temptation and malevolence. Love enables us to perceive the benevolence and compassion that God offers us in times of error or when we fall short. Love assists us in transcending the inherent shame of our deeds, enabling us to acknowledge them as valuable lessons conducive to our personal development.

The query was posed by the Apostle Paul, as he inquired, "By what means shall we be distanced from the unfailing love bestowed upon us by Christ?" (Romans 8:35 KJV). After carefully examining a comprehensive list, Paul arrived at the unequivocal determination that there is absolutely nothing capable of severing the bond between us and the benevolence of Christ. However, it is a harsh reality that a distressing incident experienced by an individual can lead to a sense of detachment from the divine affection of God.

Throughout my extensive tenure in offering pastoral assistance to individuals undergoing mental health care within psychiatric facilities, it became evident that their ailments primarily stemmed from various forms of loss, encompassing the demise of a person, an animal, aspirations, ideals, belief systems, or physical capabilities. The individuals were uprooted from the source that bestowed significance and direction to their existence. The demise (estrangement) also brought with it unaddressed ire and sorrow.

After conducting extensive research back in 1981 at Saint Elizabeths Hospital, a reputable psychiatric institution situated in Washington, D.C., I made a profound realization. I found that depression represents an internalized phenomenon wherein individuals harbor suppressed anger, which progressively erodes their vitality and overall well-being.

A considerable number of individuals are experiencing profound anguish, intense distress, and grappling with numerous letdowns to such an extent that their inner emotional turmoil of sorrow and resentment is causing detrimental effects on their well-being. What are the underlying factors that inhibit your ability to experience love due to your grief? What are the grief-related obstacles that impede you from embracing vulnerability, developing faith, and demonstrating generosity? What latent pains reside deep within your being, akin to a dormant volcano anticipating upheaval? What might be the manifestation if you were to permit your anger to emerge and become visible under the illumination of daylight? What disguise do you don as you conceal your emotions? What underlying frustration pushes you to such an extreme, where you consider the prospect of committing homicide or inflicting severe harm upon others or yourself?

Jesus entered the temple premises, actively expelled the money changers from their designated spaces employing a whip, subsequently causing the tables to overturn. I am bold enough to assert that Jesus harbored a degree of displeasure, which he conveyed by means of his conduct.

The inquiry thus arises as to how the practice of meditation can facilitate the harnessing of anger, channeling its energy, and subsequently liberating it in a manner that yields beneficial outcomes. According to the teachings of Confucius, wisdom can be acquired through three different approaches: contemplation, which is considered the most honorable; emulation, which is the most straightforward; and personal experience, which is often marked by hardships and challenges."

Meditation facilitates the acquisition of sagacity and enlightenment by means of introspective contemplation. The elderly individuals possessed a proverbial expression that goes, "Through the experiences of adversity, one gains invaluable knowledge and wisdom." An ounce of prevention is better than a pound of cure."

During a sermon, an individual proclaimed, "The inner realm of consciousness plays a pivotal role in shaping external realities." Through the practice of meditation, the divine qualities of God facilitate the attainment of enlightenment, establishing comprehension that even the act of terminating the life of a fly or an ant constitutes the extinguishment of a living being. Each of us bears a certain level of culpability for acts that result in loss of life, some of which we can reconcile and accept, while others we find intolerable.

Through the practice of meditation, individuals gain an understanding of the fundamental principles that govern our realm of existence, particularly the earthly realm and the various domains pertaining to God's virtues. Love abides by its own set of rules and must be expressed prudently during moments of introspection as we gain cognizance of our thoughts.

By intentionally and methodically confronting our grief and anger, and comprehending their capacity to confine us, we empower ourselves to both accept love and effectively harness its force in our interactions with others. It is practiced during meditation sessions as well as in moments of mindfulness throughout our daily lives.

The heart chakra, also referred to as the fourth chakra, serves as an intermediary linking three adjacent chakras. The river of affection serves as the unifying force among them all. The notion to which the Apostle Paul made reference becomes apparent in his discourse regarding faith, hope, and love, wherein love emerges as the preeminent virtue. If he possessed all things yet lacked love, his efforts were rendered fruitless. Following the resurrection of Jesus, subsequent to aiding Peter and the other disciples in their successful fishing expedition, Jesus posed the inquiry, "Peter, do you harbor affection for me?" This query was repeated threefold by Jesus. In the Gospel of John, chapter 21, verses 15-17, it is relayed that Jesus initially instructed the individual to provide sustenance to my young sheep, and on subsequent occasions, to provide nourishment to my adult sheep. (King James Version)

I had the opportunity to attend a sermon delivered by Reverend Norsworthy from Mount Moriah Baptist Church during a revival event held at First Baptist Church (Lauderdale). The sermon focused on the topic of "And Peter," incorporating the biblical verse, "But go, tell his disciples and Peter, He is going ahead of you into Galilee" (Mark 16:7 NIV).

The inquiry was presented by Reverend Norsworthy regarding the rationale behind the messenger's inclusion of the phrase "and Peter." Can it not be established that Peter was indeed one of the disciples of Jesus and that Jesus himself entrusted Peter with the authority symbolized by the keys to the kingdom? Reverend Norsworthy highlighted that Peter experienced a profound sense of disillusionment and personal inadequacy subsequent to his three-fold denial of Jesus.

Had Mary communicated that Jesus desired his disciples to convene with him in Galilee, Peter would have abstained from going. Jesus had necessitated the act of vociferating Peter's appellation in order to assure Peter of His unwavering presence and steadfast commitment. Jesus demonstrated love. Peter experienced love. Peter was compelled to distribute and nourish God's people with the same affection he had received from Jesus. The divine love that Peter encountered was destined to be transmuted into a love of the worldly nature. Love, in regards to the other chakras, serves as the conduit that must nourish and attend to each of them.

The Law of Correspondence, as per the Hermetic Principle, operates universally and governs all realms of existence. It operates in accordance with its own set of regulations. Love abides by its own set of regulations. There are individuals who assert that the heart possesses a distinct cognitive center known as the intrinsic cardiac nervous system.

It is imperative that we cultivate love within ourselves, a love that knows no conditions. This holds significance as it grants us the chance to be entrusted with the responsibility of turning the subsequent key.

The Principles And Rationale Underlying The Practice Of Meditation

The scientific mechanisms underlying the functioning of meditation are quite intriguing.

How

Once you embark on the practice of training the mind to be consciously attentive or aware, specifically by dedicating yourself to observing a single aspect of 'being' for a predetermined duration, it inevitably alters your natural state of mind. The human mind can operate in five distinct primary brainwave patterns, each characterized by a specific frequency measured in hertz, contingent upon the nature of the cognitive stimuli it is currently processing.

Gamma state: Characterized by a frequency range of 30-100Hz, the gamma state is typically observed in individuals who are actively engaged in the process of learning and assimilating novel information. The excessive activation of this condition is the root cause of hyperactivity, stress, anxiety, pervasive discontentment, and profound unhappiness.

Beta state: This brainwave state corresponds to a frequency range of 13-30Hz. Given its strong correlation with the prefrontal cortex, the brain region responsible for engaged planning, cognitive processes, and decision-making, it is common for our minds to function within the beta state of consciousness. Excessive stimulation of this mental state is unfavorable.

Alpha state: This particular state pertains to a brainwave frequency range of 9-13Hz. It is commonly encountered when engaging in activities or experiencing moments of profound relaxation, introspection, or the practice of visualizations conducive to creativity. This mental state results in an amplified sense of tranquility and a heightened feeling of being anchored and engaged.

Theta state: The theta state corresponds to a neural oscillation frequency range of 4 to 8Hz. During periods of meditation, heightened awareness of the present moment, or intentional focus on current activities, our cognitive state enters the realm of theta frequencies. When in this particular state, the mind exhibits heightened awareness, consciousness, and intuitiveness.

Delta state: Characterized by a brainwave frequency ranging from 1 to 3Hz, the delta state represents the utmost level of brainwave relaxation attainable. Our mental condition assumes this state during profound and undisturbed sleep, deep contemplation, or when we wholeheartedly immerse ourselves in an activity which we refer to as 'flow.' This mental state can also be cultivated through the regular practice of meditation, enabling us to attain a profound meditative state characterized by impartial and heightened awareness.

During the act of meditation, the brain undergoes a transition from functioning within the higher frequencies of brainwave activity (beta and alpha) to functioning within the lower frequencies: alpha, theta, and delta, ultimately achieving a state of profound meditation.

This transition results in alterations to multiple brain regions, as well as the cognitive processes involved in generating neurons and forming neuronal patterns. For instance, when the mind shifts into lower brainwave frequencies, an increased level of consciousness regarding one's thoughts and emotions arises. This heightened awareness, accompanied by a deliberate examination of thoughts in the current moment, fosters a greater degree of self-awareness and self-understanding.

In order to deepen comprehension, we shall examine the mechanisms by which meditation influences stress and anxiety, and elucidate its capacity to foster a state of greater happiness.

Why

Unintentionally, delving into the mechanisms and merits of meditation naturally steers us towards an exploration of its profound impact on different facets of existence. We will commence by examining the impact of meditation on stress levels.

Number: Alleviation of stress and anxiety

Regular meditation exerts a significant impact on the manner in which your mind and body manage stress (and anxiety). Stress and anxiety are characterized by heightened levels of physiological and psychological activation. When you express that you feel stressed, you are essentially implying that your cognitive processes are exhibiting excessive activity or hyperactivity, which could be attributed to the tendency to magnify potential negative outcomes in the future (what if scenarios) or dwell on distressing past events or memories (manifesting as regret or guilt).

When experiencing feelings of stress or anxiety, one's heart rate accelerates, as does their blood pressure and respiratory rate. Furthermore, continuous stress and anxiety elicit heightened functionality in the adrenal glands, which are responsible for the synthesis of various hormones, including cortisol, commonly known as the stress hormone. When there is an excessive secretion of cortisol by the adrenal glands, it gives rise to a hormonal imbalance that subsequently manifests as chronic stress and anxiety, accompanied by various symptoms such as agitation, migraines, disrupted sleep, hypertension, and depression.

Upon establishing a consistent meditation practice, individuals may experience a favorable impact on the activity of their sympathetic nervous system. This is due to the instructional nature of meditation, which guides the mind to transition from hyperactive states to more measured states, ultimately leading to the regulation of the stress response. When the level of stimulation in the stress response diminishes, the body reaches a state of serene tranquility, resulting in a relaxed and engaged mental state.

Meditation additionally diminishes stress (as well as anxiety, if we consider its relationship), in the subsequent manner. Engaging in a state of focused awareness and conscious presence, whether directed towards the present moment or any other specific element, has the effect of inducing a deceleration of mental processes. Consequently, this activation triggers the parasympathetic system, also referred to as the rest and digest system.

During the operation of this system, your heart rate and blood pressure decrease, leading to a state of tranquility and profound physical and mental wellness. Furthermore, the activation of this state elicits the liberation of beneficial neurotransmitters such as dopamine and serotonin. The augmentation in the secretion of these hormones facilitates advancements in cognitive acuity, concentration, and composure, correspondingly.

- Increased levels of attentiveness and concentration.

As previously stated, stress and anxiety can be described as heightened states of being. In these states, one's mind is teeming with a flurry of activity, encompassing thoughts, emotions, and various other cognitive processes. Moreover, your life might seem excessively burdensome due to the concurrent pursuit of multiple endeavors.

By providing the mind with an exercise in deliberate attention, or more precisely, by channeling the mind's focus and energy towards conscious observation of a single entity, there is a noticeable transformation in the functioning of the mind. It stands to reason that when one directs their mental focus towards a particular facet of existence over a designated duration, they develop the ability to cultivate consciousness of numerous matters while remaining fully absorbed and attentive to a singular objective.

As the intellect develops the ability to sustain consciousness and attentiveness to singular matters, the state of hyperactivity diminishes. Consequently, the mind gains enhanced capacity to exhibit attentiveness and concentration towards the exquisiteness of the current moment, the present."

#: Enhanced tranquility, contentment, and overall welfare

Meditation enhances an individual's tranquility, contentment, and overall wellness by facilitating a transition of the mind into a heightened state of engagement commonly referred to as flow.

As per the findings of Dr. Mihaly Csíkszentmihályi, renowned author of the book "Flow: The Psychology of Happiness," individuals experience an elevated state of objective happiness and overall well-being when they attain a mental state known as "flow." This state of heightened consciousness and wholehearted involvement can be attained during various activities, regardless of their nature.

Both the practice of meditation and entering a state of flow stimulate and enhance the function of the caudate nucleus within the brain. This particular region governs various cognitive processes such as learning, attention, cognition, memory, and conscious involvement. Enhanced brain functionality, elevated wellbeing, and heightened self-awareness are facilitated when this aspect of the cognitive domain is strengthened and actively engaged.

By cultivating higher consciousness and deepening your engagement with the current moment or a particular facet of it, you can experience heightened attentiveness and reduced restlessness. Consequently, your mind gains a propensity for greater introspection, enabling the discovery and apprehension of previously unfamiliar and concealed realms that would have otherwise eluded your conscious awareness. Enhanced self-awareness results in a heightened capacity to experience a sense of control, thereby reducing anxiety and fostering a greater sense of tranquility and purpose. Purposefulness in one's intentions and actions is synonymous with mindfulness, which involves effectively engaging with and making use of the present moment.

Now that we have gained a more comprehensive comprehension of meditation, its operational mechanisms, and its ability to cultivate stress relief, reduce anxiety, and promote overall happiness, let us proceed to explore seven distinct meditation techniques that can be implemented to alleviate stress and anxiety effectively, thus facilitating elevated levels of well-being.

Advantages Of Meditation Practice

The practice of meditation is associated with several advantageous outcomes. Meditation contributes to the enhancement of both physical and mental well-being, thereby facilitating the attainment of utmost bliss and fulfillment in one's existence. You will gradually gain an awareness of the immense joy that permeates your life, and the inherent capacity you possess to share this joy with those in your vicinity. And please bear in mind, meditation is not contingent upon time - a mere few minutes of your day will suffice, and rest assured, we all possess ample time to engage in any pursuit of our choosing. This is an additional advantage of engaging in meditation; it fosters the realization that one possesses ample time and that distressing over deadlines does not yield happiness, whereas completing tasks in a positive and contented manner does.

Allow us to examine the advantages attained through the practice of meditation -

Health Benefits

The majority of health problems stem either directly or indirectly from the level of stress encountered in contemporary society. Whether it be the burdens of work or the constraints of financial obligations, our relentless pursuit of success often leads us astray from reflecting upon the utmost importance of life's fundamental aspects. We increasingly direct our attention towards resolving our afflictions, consequently exacerbating our levels of stress and exacerbating various health complications.

Meditation is the most effective remedy for stress and its associated complications. The primary reason for this is that stress primarily pertains to one's mental state rather than one's physical condition. Certainly, adhering to a diet that emphasizes health and nourishment can serve as a means to prevent stress. However, it is indisputable that stress is fundamentally a psychological affliction. Through the diligent pursuit of meditation, one is able to relinquish the burdensome distractions that permeate their existence, thus facilitating the provision of the invaluable peace and respite that their mind yearns for. It enables the exertion of control over one's thoughts and mind, facilitating the ability to deactivate them when necessary, thereby refreshing the mind.

Upon establishing a consistent meditation practice, you will commence observing a marked reduction in apprehension towards life's continuous adversities. Rather, consider them as prospects that can be utilized to enhance the fulfillment in your life. Meditation instills positive qualities within your mind and body, consequently facilitating optimal performance in all aspects of your life, free from the burdens of stress.

Medical science has substantiated the claims regarding the positive effects of meditation on the overall functioning of the nervous system. This is achieved through the reduction of stress-induced chemical compounds and the promotion of the synthesis of mood-boosting enzymes such as serotonin.

In addition to enhancing the function of the nervous system and subsequently alleviating stress, meditation exerts beneficial effects on various physiological systems within the body. It has the potential to reduce blood pressure levels, while simultaneously enhancing immune system function. It is likely that you are aware of the fact that your immune system is intricately linked to your overall well-being, and that various health concerns such as allergies and lifestyle-related issues can be attributed to the manner in which you lead your life. In the event that one leads a lifestyle characterized by an absence of stressors and negative emotional experiences, it is highly probable that they will not encounter any health complications pertaining to their immune system. Conversely, should you consistently experience anxiety regarding the events unfolding in your life, it is likely that you are precipitating an inequilibrium within your immune system, consequently giving rise to a deceptive reaction - a prevalent manifestation associated with allergies. Hence, through the consistent practice of meditation, it is possible to eliminate detrimental emotions and consequently enable your body to respond positively to any circumstance, thus securing the attainment of a robust immune system as a consequential benefit.

An additional noteworthy advantage derived from consistently engaging in meditation is the decrease in one's bodily cholesterol levels. Many individuals may not be aware of this fact, but it is important to note that our bodies typically contain two distinct forms of cholesterol: the beneficial variety that is necessary for optimal bodily function, and the detrimental type that is known to contribute to various cardiovascular ailments. We are discussing the unfavorable one in this context. Through the regular practice of meditation, one can effectively maintain optimal levels of low-density lipoprotein, commonly known as bad cholesterol, within the body. This, in turn, significantly diminishes the likelihood of succumbing to any form of cardiovascular ailment. Nevertheless, for individuals currently experiencing any form of cardiac ailment, it is imperative to continue seeking proper medical attention, in conjunction with the exploration of meditation practices. In a short span of weeks, you will begin to observe transformations in your physique and experience a profound enhancement in your overall well-being.

The discussion thus far has concentrated on the positive effects muscles have on calming the mind, and it is worth noting that these benefits also extend to the alleviation of tension-related issues in terms of health. Whether one is suffering from an ulcer, joint pain, insomnia, or even headaches, meditation unquestionably offers a viable solution for obtaining relief from these ailments. Not only does meditation offer respite from these aforementioned issues, but it also guarantees to shield you from encountering any health ailments throughout your lifetime.

Another intriguing study reveals that individuals who engage in meditation experience the activation of a variety of genes responsible for combating diseases. These genes engage in combat against diseased cells and safeguard the body from cancer, ranging from the process of inflammation to cellular eradication. Through the regular practice of meditation, one can also activate the genes within the body. Therefore, this represents yet another significant health advantage derived from the practice of meditation.

Meditation additionally contributes to the maintenance of a healthy blood pressure level. Stress and anxiety have a direct impact on blood pressure. Stress is intricately connected to our primal sense of peril. Therefore, when your body detects a threat, it automatically enters a state of heightened readiness for survival, characterized by an increase in heart rate and a surge in blood pressure. Subsequently, there is a subsequent contraction of muscles and tissues, resulting in the body's negligence of the immune system and digestive system, thereby giving rise to various health complications.

Meditation, however, enables one to regulate this state of peril and guides individuals into a state of tranquility and pleasure. Hence, the maintenance of a normal heart rate and blood pressure ensures the proper functioning of your immune and digestive systems, thereby sustaining your overall health and well-being. It is as straightforward as that.

Establishing a Non-Conventional Schedule to Accommodate Meditation

Do any of the following inquiries resonate with you?

It has come to my attention that you have initiated the practice of meditation, yet you encounter challenges in allocating time for it.
Are you intending to commence your meditation sessions, yet uncertain about your ability to allocate sufficient time? Or

That you commenced your meditation practice, yet discontinued due to a lack of availability. If an affirmative response is provided to any of these inquiries, this chapter contains content of relevance to you.

The passage of time poses a significant impediment for contemporary practitioners of meditation. One could become occupied to such an extent that the sole available time at one's residence is devoted solely to acquiring restorative slumber. Nonetheless, certain individuals employ the notion of time as a justification for their inability to engage in meditation. It is ironical that occasionally, on a subconscious level, one is aware of self-deception in claiming busyness, yet continues to employ time as a pretext in order to rationalize one's actions.

Simultaneously, you allocate ample time to repeatedly peruse your Instagram account, actively update your Facebook profile on five separate occasions, as well as indulge in an additional half hour of repose by intermittently silencing your alarm clock in the mornings. Didn't you? If that is indeed the situation you find yourself in, you are employing time as a justification.

Despite the constraints of a packed schedule, wherein leisure time is scarce, it remains imperative not to allow such circumstances to impede the practice of meditation. Therefore, once you have made the decision to engage in meditation, let no obstacles impede your progress in realizing this intention. Were you aware that it is possible to engage in a meditative practice while awaiting the arrival of a train or bus, while being trapped in a traffic jam, during the act of taking a shower, or even while situated on a bench? In light of this, should you find yourself seldom afforded the opportunity to be present in the confines of your own abode, I implore you not to relinquish your commitment to the practice of meditation. Meditation can be practiced at any location and at any moment.

Meditation routine
Seasoned practitioners recommend establishing a consistent meditation practice for optimal results. In a manner akin to our customary practice of consuming breakfast in the morning, lunch at midday, and supper in the evening, this identical principle seamlessly applies to individuals engaged in the practice of meditation. If it is agreeable to you, I kindly suggest allocating some time in the morning, immediately following awakening, to

collaborate effectively. Engaging in this activity will result in feelings of contentment, tranquility, and vitality that will accompany you throughout the day. Once a routine is established, the body becomes accustomed to the program, causing noticeable differences when a session is skipped.

How to allocate sufficient time for engaging in meditation sessions
The subsequent suggestions are relevant and beneficial for establishing meditation as a consistent practice.
Carpe diem and noctem "
If it proves difficult to find time for meditation during the day, it is recommended to arise early in the morning and engage in a session. Alternatively, one may choose to meditate prior to sleep as a means of inducing relaxation.

Establish objectives for every session, and ensure their inclusion within your calendar.

According to research findings, when an individual who engages in meditation establishes specific goals for their sessions, they are more likely to adhere to the practice consistently and effectively track their advancement. Potential objectives for a session may encompass cultivating a state of relaxation, managing anger issues, enhancing one's overall well-being, or bolstering cognitive resilience.

Notify a personal acquaintance about your program.

If you are encountering difficulty in engaging with meditation, consider enlisting the support of a trusted individual to motivate and assist you in persevering along this transformative path. It could be your spouse, significant other, or a close family member such as a parent. By informing them about your program, they will consistently keep you accountable, inquire about your progress, and if you ever contemplate skipping sessions, they can serve as a valuable source of motivation and support.

Choose a designated area for the practice of meditation.

If it is possible for you to engage in meditation within the confines of your own abode, it would be advisable to designate a specific area within your dwelling for this purpose. Furnish this space with a plush armchair, an ornate vase filled with flowers, a container of fragrant incense, a tastefully lit candle, and a soft carpet to enhance your meditative experience. Once you imbue the location with sacredness, it will serve as the epitome of a profound reminder.

Track your time

At times, it is crucial to subject oneself to challenges in order to ascertain the availability of sufficient time. By evaluating your timetable, it will be feasible to determine opportune moments for incorporating meditation.

You will also have the opportunity to pose these inquiries to yourself:

- What is the duration of my sleep? Do they exceed the required amount?
- For what duration should I engage in viewing movies, series, or television programs?
- To what extent have I dedicated my time to socializing with my friends?
- What is the time difference between my waking up and my reporting to work?
- Can I momentarily deactivate my morning alarm?

By responding to these inquiries, you will ascertain whether you are employing time as a justification.

Take advantage of any available moment of your free time.

In the event of a limited availability of time, it is still possible to engage in the practice of meditation, albeit in alternative locations and during non-conventional hours.

For example,

- Upon the completion of your workday and prior to commuting, allocate 10 minutes of your time to engage in the practice of meditation before returning to your residence.
- In the event that you possess a lunch break lasting for one hour, it remains possible for you to engage in meditation prior to consuming your meal. Identify a suitable and cost-free area within your office premises to establish a designated space for meditation purposes.

- Should you be employed in a shared workspace, kindly inform your coworkers so as to garner their consideration and acknowledgement of your need for a quiet environment.

Ultimately, there is never an instance wherein time will prove to be sufficient. You will consistently perceive your internal monologue urging you to unwind momentarily, as time slips by imperceptibly. So when you start meditating, time will keep appearing like an obstacle. It remains evident that meditation is accessible to individuals regardless of their daily routines, be it a fixed schedule or sporadic availability. It is not necessary for your sessions to be of a duration of 20 minutes; even brief sessions lasting just 5 minutes can yield remarkable results. It is not obligatory to engage in meditation when one is at home, thereby allowing for the flexibility to meditate at any given time and in any location.

Visualizing

Meditation often includes visualizations. Visualizing means imagining. When engaging in visualization, you direct your cognitive faculties towards generating a particular creation. One has the ability to mentally depict their objectives, an impactful visual representation, or any subject matter that one deems significant to concentrate on.

The images you create in your mind will significantly impact you, therefore exercise discretion in selecting your aspirations. As an illustration, should you desire to enhance the state of mental tranquility during your relaxation practice, one effective approach would be to conceive of a serene setting, such as a sunset, that evokes a sense of calmness. To alleviate the impact of a troubling memory, one may modify its portrayal in the mind to invoke humor or ennui (by incorporating a soundtrack, imbuing characters with ludicrous actions, visualizing it monochromatically).

Visualizations are among the instrumental resources at one's disposal that can be employed to alter one's cognitive and emotional perspective towards various matters. Engage in these experiments to acquire insights into the transformative potential of deliberate thinking.

Writing

Writing can serve as a means of engaging in contemplative expression. Through writing, you can release your pent-up emotions and process them. One is free to engage in communication with whomever or whatever they desire: be it a cherished individual, an ongoing endeavor, or a divine entity. You have the option to transmit the content you have composed to a recipient, retain it privately, or dispose of it. It is not necessary for anyone else to read it in order for it to be effective.

Compose without constraint and endeavor to abstain from making revisions - in doing so, you will facilitate the emergence of your subconscious thoughts. Utilize this period to release any concerns or burdens that are weighing on you. Once you have completed your task, ensure to peruse and internalize the contents of your composition. Reflect on it. Expressing your emotions through the act of writing facilitates a fresh and altered outlook on the matter at hand.

Dealing with Distressing Feelings

One can employ the practice of meditation to enhance the capacity to manage emotions effectively. One may opt to select their emotions as the focal point for their meditation practice. Embrace their inherent qualities without subjecting them to thorough examination or alteration. Merely experiencing the emotions without augmenting their intensity through heightened sensory perception or resisting them serves to diminish their impact.

Maintain a state of tranquility and composure by adopting conscious control over your breathing. Remind yourself, "I am experiencing (emotion), however, I am not defined by my (emotion)." Engaging in this practice with your undesired emotions will progressively diminish their influence on you.

Detachment Exercise

Meditation possesses the capacity to enhance one's presence of mind (thus fostering mindfulness) while simultaneously aiding in the cultivation of emotional detachment. The state of detachment facilitates the restoration of mental clarity and enhances one's ability to exercise control.

In the event that you find yourself confronted with a problem, exert conscious effort to disengage from it. Adopt a perspective from an external observer, and envision a different individual placed in your current circumstances. This enables you to gain a fresh outlook on your predicament and assess with composure and reasonability the necessary course of action.

Close your eyes. Take into consideration the circumstances that are causing you distress. Visualize the scenario as if it were being projected onto a screen situated before you. Observe the occurrences on the display, yet engage in the action that truly transpired rather than indulging apprehensions of possible events. Substitute your presence with that of another individual. In your capacity as an external observer, what counsel would you offer to the individual appearing on the screen? Please bear in mind and proceed in accordance with the counsel you have provided.

One can cultivate a greater level of detachment by altering the mental representation of any given matter. By adopting an external vantage point, one can cultivate a capacity to react in an altered manner.

Additionally, you have the option to engage your subconscious mind to tackle the issue. Release your grip on it and direct your attention towards another matter. The resolution may be obtained in the upcoming instance of your meditation practice, during a state of mind characterized by receptivity.

Encouraging Success

The objects of your attention possess the power to influence your behaviors; therefore, direct your focus towards something that is constructive and uplifting. If you encounter a challenge, envision projecting yourself into the future, to a point in time when the issue has already been resolved. Immerse yourself in an experiential understanding of the solution. Retain the optimistic sentiments and carry them forward into the present moment.

Do not become preoccupied with the logistical details of its realization, rather, remain focused on your objective. Directing your attention towards a favorable outcome facilitates enhanced cognitive clarity, enabling you to exercise sound judgment and ultimately culminate in the achievement of your intended objectives. Should you desire, you have the option to direct your attention towards distinct objectives on a daily basis, as long as you cultivate a mindset conducive to continual advancement.

Focusing on a Idea

Engaging in contemplation of a concept facilitates a more thorough assimilation of its content. Close your eyes. Select a term that embodies an aspired condition: clarity, harmony, bliss, competence, peace, or relaxation. Additionally, one can generate cognitive visualizations to elucidate the concept. Envision the sensation one might encounter upon encountering the aforementioned condition. Once you have accomplished this, endeavor to maintain it for as an extended period as possible. Open your eyes. When the need arises to reenter that state, recollect the sensory impressions and insights that were acquired in the course of your meditation.

Mental Relaxation

Your mental state can experience a sense of tranquility by actively relinquishing any sources of distress and directing your attention towards your desired objective. Furthermore, it is possible to mentally envisage concepts that facilitate a heightened state of relaxation and deep immersion.

As stated in the preceding exercise, it is possible to engage in contemplation regarding one's perception of relaxation. Additionally, one can envision engaging in an act that serves as a representation of their heightened state of consciousness.

Which activity or practice induces a state of inner tranquility for you? Does it involve descending or ascending? Repetitive motions? Floating? Here is an exercise that you can use or modify to relax more fully.

Close your eyes. Count back from 100-1. Upon reaching the numerical value of 1, envision the presence of a staircase directly ahead of your position. Examine the staircase from your own perspective, rather than relying on the viewpoint of someone external. Proceed to descend upon it and affirm to your conscious self that with each step down, you are delving further and further into the depths of your own psyche.

Another option is to utilize an elevator. Observe the correlation between a decrease in the numerical representation of the floor level and the ensuing attainment of a state of increased composure. When you reach 0, enter a room or a place that you feel absolutely good to be in. Allocate a portion of your time to being present in that area. Once you have attained a state of complete relaxation, you can then direct your attention towards your chosen focus of meditation or savor the tranquil state of meditation.

Meditation in Motion

It is possible to engage in meditation while in a state of motion. An effective approach involves synchronizing your breath with your actions. Furthermore, one can engage in dance or partake in improvisational movements in response to music. Subsequently, remain motionless and attentively focus on your breathing. This type of meditation provides liberation whenever you encounter a sense of being immobilized. It further fosters a state of equilibrium and coherence between the faculties of your physique and cognition.

One can engage in meditation while undertaking the tasks of constructing, designing, or embellishing something. One has the ability to engage in various creative pursuits such as drawing, painting, writing, or experimenting with diverse mediums. Ensure that you dedicate your undivided attention to the task at hand.

Watching Thoughts Exercise

Release yourself from any and all external distractions. Kindly shut your eyes and direct your focus towards your internal realm. To the best of your ability, impartially observe the thoughts that traverse your consciousness. Refrain from passing judgment on individuals, hold onto positive ones, and refrain from suppressing negative ones.

Observe the sequential progression of thoughts. Take note of the activities of your mind, as it has the tendency to divert your attention. Additionally, please take note of how your consciousness becomes enveloped by your cognitions. In the event of such occurrence, redirect your attention.

Knowing the Knower Exercise

Please endeavor to calm your thoughts. Observe the mental processes that traverse your consciousness without engaging with them. Reflect upon your existence and inquire, "What is my true identity?" "Who is engaged in the act of meditation?" "Who assumes the role of the observer of these thoughts?"

Please refrain from anticipating a response. Allow for the possibility of gaining insights, but refrain from imposing expectations on their arrival. The objective is not to discover a solution. The interrogation itself constitutes the fundamental purpose of the endeavor.

Should you encounter the situation where you are providing answers to your own inquiries, it is imperative to scrutinize the validity and accuracy of your responses. If your answer was,

"The individual engaged in meditation is myself within this corporeal vessel," you may proceed with a query along the lines of, "By what means do you discern that it is indeed your essence dwelling within your physical form?" and subsequently address this inquiry. Persist in pursuing this line of thought until you reach a point where you are unable to refute any further arguments that may arise.

Working with Zen Koans

A Koan refers to a perplexing inquiry that eludes resolution through logical means, instead necessitating a shift in perspective to attain understanding. This compels you to engage your cognitive faculties in previously unexplored ways. There exist commonly known koans such as the question of "what is the sound produced by a single hand clapping?"; however, a meditation instructor has the ability to provide you with a distinctive koan to engage with.

This particular meditation technique is renowned for its level of difficulty, yet it carries significant benefits for the mind. Devote yourself fully to your koan. Please refrain from making any alterations due to the difficulties you are currently experiencing. Experiencing frustration is an inherent aspect of the overall encounter.

Embracing the koan will render it more manageable, akin to embracing vexing emotions which will weaken their hold on you. Please rest assured that there is no need for you to be troubled by the inability to solve it in a timely manner. Even if the solution has not yet been attained, engaging with the koan will yield positive effects if one allows it to influence them.

Reflect upon the koan not solely in the midst of meditation, but rather frequently and consistently. Once you feel prepared, engage in a conversation with your teacher regarding your proposed solution. Should you not possess one, it is feasible to engage in solitary introspection regarding your resolution. Incorporate the knowledge gleaned from the paradox into your everyday actions.

As is evident, there exists a multitude of meditation techniques, thereby affording the flexibility to fashion a personalized regimen. The concluding section addresses the means to surmount prevalent challenges encountered while engaging in meditation and maximize the benefits obtained from every session.

Practicing Mindfulness Meditation

There exist a multitude of methods to engage in mindfulness meditation; crucially, one must strive to identify the approach that aligns most effectively with their particular way of life. I understand that life is filled with various obligations and commitments, leading to a busy schedule. Despite these demands, it is essential to allocate a small portion of time each day to engage in the practice of mindfulness meditation, in order to prevent ourselves from being overwhelmed by the incessant flow of life.

Given that mindfulness meditation involves intentionally focusing one's attention and maintaining a heightened state of awareness in the present moment, it bears a resemblance to the discipline required in mastering martial arts or a musical instrument. Engaging in skillful meditation necessitates a conscious and mindful approach.

In the context of engaging in a formal practice, typically one's attention is centered on the breath as the focal point of awareness. As the rhythmic inhalation and exhalation of our respiration permeates our being, we endeavor to diligently attend to the sensations that arise. We allow our breath to traverse our physique organically, in contrast to deliberate breathing techniques which involve regulation and even synchronization. The purpose of mindfulness meditation entails diligently attending to the sensory experience of one's breath.

It is imperative to grasp the concept that during the practice of mindfulness meditation, we frequently succumb to distractions. Various sensory experiences, emotions, thoughts, and cognitive processes vie for attention within our consciousness, leading us to inadvertently disregard the significance of our breath. However, once you come to this realization, proceed to refocus your thoughts on the breath, utilizing patience, gentleness, kindness, and a hint of curiosity towards your own being. Please keep in mind that this activity should not induce stress. Therefore, it is advisable to take pleasure in it and, above all, exercise patience.

Similar to experimentation, honing one's abilities necessitates dedication to practicing. With consistent efforts, the practice of mindfulness meditation becomes progressively more manageable. Additionally, it is beneficial to refrain from harboring any feelings of self-consciousness or passing critical judgments regarding the progression of your meditation practice. The customary approach is to calmly unwind and become aware of the present moment.

Adopting a Vertical and Relaxed Stance

As previously alluded to, there exist various approaches to engage in mindfulness meditation. However, should one seek to acquire proficiency in the ceremonial discipline, it becomes imperative to acquaint oneself with the requisite body alignment as well. It can be concluded that this task is relatively simple and uncomplicated.

Step 1

Please choose a suitable seating option, such as a park bench, meditation cushion, or any chair that offers a firm and stable place to sit. Please refrain from loitering or sitting on the chair.

Step 2

If you have elected to position yourself on a cushion placed on the floor, I would recommend assuming a posture where you comfortably rest your legs in a crossed position in front of you, resembling the traditional seating style associated with the Indian culture. Furthermore, please do not hesitate to opt for a seated yoga posture if that is your preferred method. Nevertheless, should you opt to be seated in a chair, ensure that your feet are firmly positioned on the floor in front of you.

Step 3

Maintain proper posture by aligning your upper body in a straight position. Avoid slouching, but do not overly rigid your back. Strive to sit comfortably in an upright position. Ensure that your shoulders and head are positioned in alignment with the natural contour of your spine, with both resting comfortably upon your vertebrae.

Step 4

Please ensure that your upper arms maintain a parallel alignment with your body, positioned alongside and at the sides, while your hands rest atop your legs. Please refrain from positioning your hands excessively towards the rear as it may result in a rigid demeanor. By positioning your hands significantly forward, you will assume a posture that promotes hunching. Just allow your erect posture to determine the appropriate placement of your hands on your lap in a relaxed manner.

Step 5

When meditating, you do not need to close your eyes. Many individuals find themselves in this predicament due to difficulties in maintaining focus, as they are prone to being easily distracted by their surroundings. It is possible to keep your eyes open without specifically fixating your gaze on a particular object. Kindly lower your chin slightly while directing your gaze in a gradual downward direction.

Step 6

Ensure that you adopt a comfortable stance before commencing the act of attuning your attention to each inhale and exhale, embodying a state of remorse and penitence.

Various Mindfulness Meditation Focus

The formal application of mindfulness meditation involves assuming a seated position, irrespective of your physical surroundings, provided they offer a tranquil ambiance. In adhering to the prescribed sequence of actions for attaining proper posture, proceed to establish a composed and settled position. When engaging in formal mindfulness meditation, various iterations of the technique exist, owing to the simultaneous operation of our five distinct sensory organs. Engaging in simultaneous attention to all five aspects would not align with the practice of mindfulness meditation. Therefore, mindfulness meditation is divided into five distinct facets.

Breathing

Rather than focusing on the sense of smell, the primary emphasis lies on your respiration. As you breathe in, focus on the breath as it enters your body and fills you with air, feel your chest and lungs expand. Next, direct your focus towards the exhalation of air from your lungs, observing the expansion of your abdomen and the subsequent deflation of your lungs. Be mindful of the air you breathe, is it warm, cold, does it have a distinct aroma? Enjoy each breath.

This particular exercise can readily be integrated into your daily routine, with a duration of one to three minutes being sufficient. This task can be accomplished in either a seated or upright position. In the event that you find your thoughts wandering, kindly redirect your attention towards your breathing. Exercise patience and empathy towards yourself, refraining from being harsh or critical, and avoiding self-reproach for any perceived lack of self-discipline. This activity is expected to be a pleasurable exercise that allows you to gain further understanding of yourself, your environment, and the present moment.

Thoughts

One of the primary challenges individuals often encounter when engaging in mindfulness meditation pertains to the difficulty in attaining a state of thoughtlessness, in which the mind remains devoid of any cognitive content, resulting in a blank and vacuous mental state. Indeed, it is undeniably challenging to halt the incessant flow of thoughts traversing through one's mind. However, it should be noted that nothing is insurmountable, and through diligent and regular practice, one can readily overcome these thoughts. In general, one may find it significantly challenging to clear one's thoughts, particularly when attempting to engage in meditation. It is important to note that these thoughts often become quite intense and disruptive before subsiding.

Sensations

Another aspect to direct your attention towards during your practice of mindfulness meditation involves the observation of physical sensations. This particular type of concentration proves highly advantageous in mitigating emotional distress. By directing your undivided and impartial attention to the sensory perceptions occurring both internally and externally, you can attain a state of profound meditative contemplation. Emotions are additionally regarded as internal sensations experienced within oneself. It entails introspecting on one's emotions and their underlying causes. Engage in introspection to understand the underlying causes and mechanisms that give rise to these emotions within yourself. This approach offers a valuable opportunity to cultivate objectivity and assess misplaced emotions. This constitutes a compelling explanation as to why mindfulness meditation serves as an effective stress management tool. Through this practice, individuals are afforded the opportunity to thoroughly analyze their emotions and engage in self-dialogue aimed at relinquishing the burdensome weight of such emotions, as they often possess insubstantial significance.

Sounds

For certain individuals, optimal meditation occurs within a tranquil setting. However, it should be noted that sounds can also serve as a central focus during the practice of mindfulness meditation. Consider, for instance; the act of listening to the resonant waves can be an exquisite, tranquil, and rejuvenating auditory experience for a multitude of people. Discover a particular sound that provides a calming effect. This could encompass musical compositions or even the harmonious interplay of natural elements, such as the melodious trills of birds, the gentle rustling of squirrels, or the harmonious cadence of a flowing stream. Direct your attention solely towards this auditory sensation, allowing the emotions it evokes to envelop you completely.

Taste

Indeed, the aspect of taste serves as an excellent point of focus during your mindfulness meditation practice. After all, who does not hold an appreciation for the culinary arts? However, have you been conscious of the dietary choices you have been making? Have you ever attempted to analyze and deconstruct the distinct elements encompassing the flavors, textures, and temperature that composed your most recent dining experience? Probably not. Therefore, it is evident that a substantial amount of valuable insights were forfeited as you hastily consumed your food without contemplation. Additionally, this approach can be employed to fully appreciate your meals and may serve as a useful technique to prevent excessive consumption.

Traditional And Integrative Methods For Promoting Wellness

The ramifications of the classical paradigm, which posited a dichotomy between the realm of the mind and matter, in which both are perceived as completely autonomous entities, have become starkly evident within the realm of healthcare. Traditional Western medicine has traditionally perceived the human body as a complex system, wherein the defective components require fixing or substitution once they malfunction. These distinct components are attended to by specialized practitioners, frequently with minimal consideration for the holistic nature of the organism. Despite the advancement of Western medicine in the realm of treating physical disease symptoms, there has been limited emphasis on the influential role of mental processes, emotional attitudes, as well as social and environmental factors in the etiology of illnesses.

Advanced surgical techniques and the progress in chemotherapy, the primary modalities of traditional medicine, have not only preserved numerous lives but also mitigated extensive suffering and agony. Furthermore, these tools find application in the therapeutic management of mental disorders and exhibit notable efficacy in symptom regulation. Nevertheless, pharmaceutical substances frequently exhibit detrimental toxic effects, leading to additional complexities, and potentially compromising their intended efficacy. As an illustration, when considering the instance of mental illness, pharmaceutical interventions serve to alleviate symptoms rather than provide a cure, since they fail to address the underlying psychological factors contributing to the disorder. In the grand scheme, this can only have counterproductive effects. Despite the impressive advancements witnessed in modern medicine, a notable shortcoming lies in its limited and mechanistic perception of the human body. Moreover, the modalities employed for treatment frequently neglect the patient's intrinsic capacity for self-recovery and their personal accountability for their state of well-being.

Alternative modalities for health and wellness, such as acupuncture or homeopathy, exhibit a perspective that aligns more closely with the conceptual framework of reality emerging from contemporary physics and as apprehended by individuals with mystical inclinations. These methodologies are frequently referred to as 'holistic' due to their perspective on the individual as a cohesive entity, wherein all its constituent elements are interconnected and interdependent, a concept derived from the Greek term 'halos' meaning 'whole'. The integrity of the entirety would be compromised if any component were to be harmed or extracted. Alternative therapies acknowledge the interrelation between the mind, body, and spirit, and duly consider the reciprocal influence and impact of mental and physical conditions on one another. Therefore, illness is perceived as a disruption or state of imbalance of the entire being, rather than being attributed to a singular factor, such as a malfunction within a specific component of the physical body.

There exist numerous approaches towards holistic treatment, although the majority entail minimal intervention with the organism aimed at harnessing the inherent self-healing capacity, in contrast to the interventional methods employed in conventional medicine. In juxtaposition with the conventional framework for addressing illnesses, whereby the doctor assumes full responsibility, a holistic approach necessitates the individual to assume personal accountability for the treatment and prevention of diseases through the adoption of a wholesome lifestyle encompassing nutrition, physical activity, relaxation, and meditation. Scientific evidence has emerged to substantiate the psycho-physiological advantages of meditation, predominantly attributed to its capacity to alleviate stress.

Stress

A considerable amount of information and literature pertaining to stress has been disseminated in recent times, leading to a widespread awareness and general understanding of this phenomenon among the majority of individuals. Nevertheless, the terminology is employed with a high degree of ambiguity and primarily linked to circumstances and events that engender unease and hardship.

What is stress?

The term 'stress' was initially employed in the field of physics to denote a force that exerts itself upon an object, ultimately engendering or predisposing it to undergo deformation or strains. Furthermore, it is employed to define the condition of an object within these circumstances. The level of deformation or strain experienced by the object due to the applied force will be contingent upon its capacity to bear loads, its flexibility, and its tolerance. If the object exhibits the ability to regain its original shape or form upon the cessation of external forces, it is referred to as possessing elasticity. Conversely, if the object sustains its deformed state and fails to recover its original shape, it is characterized as being plastic. If an elastic band is stretched and subsequently released, it will revert back to its initial form. If subjected to excessive strain, the material will endure lingering deformation even once the external force is ceased, or it may experience fracture.

When it comes to living organisms, stress can be described as a condition of psychophysiological stimulation triggered by social, physical, and emotional elements, specifically those that pose a threat or necessitate adjustment or adaptation. The subsequent explanation will cover the physiological alterations that coincide with this reaction, commonly identified as the 'fight or flight response'. The term 'stress' may also encompass the external pressures or conditions that impact the organism, thereby triggering this adaptive reaction.

Stress as an indispensable element of existence

Stress is commonly perceived as an ominous specter that looms over individuals' existence and ought to be diligently evaded. However, it should be noted that momentary stress plays a vital role in human existence, as it enables individuals to effectively navigate and adapt to their surroundings. An instance of this can be seen in the vital biological stress mechanism, which plays a crucial role in facilitating the fundamental human instincts of procreation and survival. It is imperative for athletes to experience a state of anxiousness prior to a race in order to optimize their performance. It is completely normal to experience stress reactions such as feelings of anxiety prior to a significant decision, sensations of tension before public performance, or a sense of fear when faced with a threatening situation. They constitute an integral aspect of the organic mechanisms that the body employs to adapt and respond to demanding circumstances, facilitating optimal coping strategies for individuals.

Stress permeates every facet of our endeavors, for it is in the absence of stress that stagnation prevails, depriving us of the dynamism, innovation, and zest that imbue our lives. Individuals would find themselves incapable of fulfilling any of the expectations placed upon them, thereby negating any potential for personal development. The deleterious effects of stress manifest only when it is prolonged or excessive, and when the energy generated by the stress response remains unexpended, thereby contributing significantly to the occurrence of diseases.

What causes stress?

There is a diverse range of stimuli that can elicit the stress response. Significant life upheavals such as the loss of a loved one, marital separation, financial difficulties, or academic evaluations serve as evident catalysts for stressful experiences. Additional factors that impact individuals to varying extents encompass environmental and social elements, namely air and noise pollution, urban congestion, and the quality of living and working environments. Work-related challenges often serve as prevalent and significant catalysts of stress. The exasperation and discontentment brought about by employment positions that lack intellectual stimulation, monotonous duties, or sheer tedium can generate a level of stress equivalent to that of meeting deadlines, managing pressures, shouldering excessive responsibility, or facing intense competition. Additional factors that may contribute to stress encompass interpersonal connections, socio-economic standing, the pace of life alterations, and insufficient sleep.

It is worth noting that pleasurable experiences, such as vacations, romantic relationships, or career advancements, can also induce stress, a factor that is not always widely acknowledged. Stress is a fundamental aspect of existence and is unavoidable. The eradication of the primary sources could potentially necessitate modifications in one's social circle, family dynamics, professional environment, and personal ideology – alterations that, for the majority, are impractical and unappealing. It is possible, however, to manage the level of stress in one's life and mitigate the excessive burden that could lead to significant harm to the individual.

Stress overload

Stress can be likened to an electrical current flowing within a circuit. The circuit has been specifically engineered to maintain a predetermined level of electrical current, as its functionality is contingent upon the presence of this essential requirement. However, in the event that the electrical current surpasses its capacity and the circuit becomes excessively burdened, there is a risk of overheating or tripping the fuse. Likewise, an individual whose capacity to tolerate stress is surpassed or who fails to manage it effectively will experience agitation or encounter a disruptive reaction. In the realm of mechanical systems, it is a well-known fact that the component with the least strength or resilience will invariably be the initial point of failure. This principle extends to biological processes, whereby a deficiency in the cardiac function may culminate in a heart attack, or a compromised stomach function may prompt the development of an ulcer. Certain individuals experience a cognitive disturbance which induces a state of extreme psychological distress and leads to a significant breakdown of their mental well-being. Individuals exhibit significant variations in their capacity to endure stress, as certain individuals, particularly those in positions of leadership like politicians, may flourish and derive satisfaction from elevated stress levels, while others experience an abrupt breakdown even in the face of minor annoyances.

Signs that stress has escalated to detrimental levels can manifest through emotional, behavioral, or physiological cues. Each individual experiences a unique combination of symptoms, however the common emotional responses to stress encompass impaired concentration, indecisiveness, diminished self-worth, despondency, apprehension, edginess, and periodic displays of intense emotion. Typical behavioral manifestations include heightened levels of smoking and alcohol consumption, fluctuations in appetite, withdrawal from social interactions, and the exhibition of physical habits like teeth grinding, nail biting, and restless tapping of the feet. Physiological manifestations encompass symptoms such as migraines, high blood pressure, sleep disturbances, abnormal respiration, cardiac disturbances, and gastrointestinal troubles. Fortunately, there exist proficient methods by which excessive stress can be mitigated, and stress levels can be prevented from reaching uncomfortable or perilous thresholds.

Fight or flight response

The physiological reaction elicited by any stress stimulus, be it genuine or perceived, pertaining to the body or mind, is scientifically referred to as the 'fight or flight' response. This reaction is analogous in humans and other animals, encompassing a intricate sequence of biochemical processes. As the term implies, these processes equip the organism for heightened activity, either engaging in intense physical confrontation or fleeing from a perceived threat.

When the fight or flight response is activated, the release of stress hormones, namely adrenaline and noradrenaline, gives rise to various physiological alterations in the body. The lungs facilitate increased oxygen intake, resulting in an accelerated heart rate and elevated blood pressure. Enhanced blood flow to the musculature of the limbs and cerebral regions facilitates improved cognitive abilities, rapid reflexes, and prompt cognitive processing. Simultaneously, the liver expels glucose and lipids into the circulatory system to offer sustenance for the muscles. The musculature assumes a taut state in anticipation of activity, while the body readies itself for thermal regulation through heightened perspiration. Physiological functions, such as digestion, come to a halt as blood flow is redirected from the skin and digestive organs. The musculature of the bowels and bladder undergoes relaxation, eliciting the sensation or urge to engage in defecation or urination.

In this heightened state of arousal, an individual is most aptly equipped to navigate and respond to challenges or potential perils. After engaging in either combat or evasion to address a threat and once the peril has dissipated, the bodily organs undergo relaxation as the system returns to its customary state of equilibrium, commonly referred to as homeostasis.

Healthy and injurious responses

The human body exhibits nearly identical reactions to any stress stimulus, albeit with nuanced variations in the released quantities of adrenaline and noradrenaline, delineating one stress response from another. Adrenaline can be regarded as the hormone associated with fear or the instinctual response to flee, whereas noradrenaline is the hormone linked to anger or the inclination to confront challenges. Noradrenaline, when mistakenly attributed to adrenaline, is accountable for the euphoric sensation that some individuals experience, thus leading to the development of a dependence on stress.

The fight or flight response was highly adapted to early humans, as their survival hinged upon their capacity to engage in physical combat or to flee. However, in contemporary society, particularly in Western cultures, the act of surviving has shifted to primarily involve engaging in job competition, securing employment, meeting rigorous productivity targets, demonstrating effective negotiation skills, and similar endeavors. The issue lies in the fact that this psychological stress gives rise to a physiological reaction. If one encounters a situation where a traffic jam ensues, resulting in the unfortunate consequence of missing an appointment, or if one were to forfeit a significant business contract, it can be concluded that the instinctual fight or flight response would be deemed unfitting in such circumstances. You are prevented from both evading and physically attacking your 'adversary', despite any inclination you may experience. If there are no socially permissible alternatives available to you, the energy generated by the stress response remains unexpended. The body continues to experience a state of imbalance and an accompanying sensation of tension persists. Moreover, should the psychological circumstances endure, the physiological stress reaction will continue as well. The accumulation of stress hormones and muscular tension persists and poses a risk to one's overall well-being.

Although the stress response is a beneficial adaptive reaction, it is also a transient condition intended to address immediate crises. Regrettably, in practical terms, the fight or flight response does not exclusively manifest in emergency circumstances. Rather, it is the recurrent occurrence of unwarranted biological alarms that ultimately result in harm. In an attempt to comprehend the distinction between adaptive and harmful stress reactions, consider envisioning a scenario wherein you find yourself crossing a road and a vehicle begins accelerating towards you, posing a significant risk of potential harm. Within a few seconds, your heart rate would nearly double and you would promptly transition into a running motion. Upon successfully reaching the opposite side of the road, it is likely that a sense of relief would surge through you. In tandem, you may feel a heightened state of exhilaration, accompanied by a noticeable trembling in your body, as your respiration returns to its regular pace and a state of relaxation gradually settles in. Analyze this response by contrasting it with the emotions experienced after a taxing day, where one is unable to recuperate between successive demands or emergencies. It is probable that your body has been experiencing continuous stimulation throughout the course of the day. The development of stress-related disorders is attributed to the extended duration of stress. In the event that the body remains in a state of reactivity without being able to dissipate the generated energy, or if the perceived threat continues to persist, or if the response is repeatedly stimulated, it is highly probable that the manifestation of an illness will occur.

Why Start Today?

One of the objectives of meditation is to progressively cultivate a state of equanimity and serenity within the mind. When the state of the mind is tranquil, one can transcend concerns and emotional unease, thereby attaining a genuine sense of joy. Nevertheless, in the absence of tranquility within one's mind, achieving happiness becomes exceedingly difficult, regardless of the favorable circumstances one may be residing in. Through the practice of meditation, one can cultivate a state of unwavering composure and resilience, even when confronted with the most challenging circumstances that life may present.

Additionally, engaging in meditation enhances one's wisdom and offers a distinct perspective. Through the process of introspection, one comes to the realization that there is no need to subject oneself to the bondage of the mind. It may exhibit emotional outbursts, experience feelings of envy, sadness, or joy, yet it should not dictate your actions. Meditation may be regarded as a practice of mental purification, encompassing the removal of any mental clutter, refinement of innate abilities, and establishing a profound connection with one's authentic essence. It resembles cleansing the mind. Consequently, you will experience heightened clarity and a broadened perspective. We may not possess the ability to exert influence over external circumstances, but we certainly possess the capacity to shape the caliber of our cognitive faculties. Regardless of your actions or circumstances, as long as your mental state remains intact, everything will undoubtedly be fine.

Regular practice is important. It is imperative to acquire proficiency in adhering to the proper meditation techniques and placing unwavering trust in them. There is no need to exert excessive effort in order to achieve this, as meditation inherently embodies the desired outcome.

It would also be prudent to deliberate on the instances wherein meditation may not be advisable. It is not advisable to participate in meditation if you are experiencing severe depression or harboring thoughts of self-harm. If you experience mild depression, it is advised that you seek the assistance of a meditation teacher or a trusted individual with whom you have a close professional relationship, in order to address your feelings of irritability. Acquiring proficiency in novel meditation techniques can present a considerable challenge. Occasionally, individuals find themselves directing their attention towards potential concerns and pitfalls. They have a tendency to hold the belief that it is not functioning properly, despite its actual functionality. Consistent guidance and constructive feedback can assist you in effectively implementing meditative techniques.

We frequently encounter challenges in calming our minds. It appears to resemble a balloon, susceptible to being influenced and carried about by external circumstances. In the event of favorable outcomes, our state of mind experiences contentment, whereas unfavorable circumstances lead to its discontentment. In the event that we acquire our desires, we experience a surge of enthusiasm and clutch onto them with firm resolve. However, as the circumstances of life often dictate, it is not always feasible to obtain the objects of our desires. Consequently, our emotional attachment to such desires inevitably results in anguish and suffering. When our desires remain unfulfilled or when we experience the loss of something dear to us, we find ourselves engulfed in a state of hopelessness and agitation.

Through the consistent practice of meditation, one can cultivate a state of mental equanimity—a poised and attentive mind that remains steadfast, as opposed to being prone to fluctuating between episodes of hyperactivity and despondency. Through regular and dedicated practice of meditation, one will eventually acquire the ability to eradicate the illusions and misconceptions that reside within the mind, thereby addressing the fundamental cause of all difficulties and distress. In this manner, you will have the opportunity to encounter an enduring state of tranquility referred to as "nirvana" or "liberation." Moreover, you will encounter a growing solidity in your existence, independent of external conditions.

Additionally, you acquire a heightened awareness and fresh perspective on the narratives generated by your own thoughts. The majority of us are simply preoccupied with inner conflicts. Upon relinquishing the negative emotions stemming from your past experiences, you initiate the unfurling of your heart, thereby discovering an expansive realm wherein you can embrace benevolence and empathy. Kindness serves as the catalyst for establishing connections among individuals, while compassion enhances not only the connections we have with others, but also fosters a deep sense of connection with ourselves and the broader world.

Meditation keeps you real. Upon gaining a deeper understanding of one's own psyche, individuals naturally cultivate a sense of genuineness, tranquility, and quite possibly, a heightened state of humility. The primary factor in effectively managing stress and discovering genuine purpose in your professional and personal relationships is to lead a life rooted in unwavering benevolence, both towards oneself and towards others. One displays their genuine talents when they act with bona fide benevolence and empathy towards others. By traversing the journey of life with impartiality towards oneself and others, one will observe the auspicious transformations in relation to their understanding and encounter of existence.

Strategies For Expediting The Process Of Falling Asleep

Facilitating Mindful Meditation for Enhanced Quality of Rest and Slumber

Welcome to your guided sleep meditation
- Set aside a brief period of time to place yourself in a positive environment, remove all electronic devices including screens such as laptops and phones.
- Recline on your properly arranged bed and comfortably position yourself under the covers, ensuring that your pillow is appropriately placed.
- As the daylight hours are drawing to a close. Embrace the nocturnal vitality and express gratitude for the events that transpired throughout the day.

Release all tense circumstances, restless thoughts, concerns, and anticipation, and permit your mind to concentrate during this serene instance.

- Meditation enhances and sustains the secretion of melatonin, the hormone that regulates the sleep initiation process, by devoting increased focus to your breathing while experiencing a state of relaxation.

- Inhale deeply, and as you release each breath, experience a growing sense of relaxation.

- You are progressively relinquishing your concerns. - Over time, you are becoming increasingly detached from your worries. - Your worries are gradually diminishing.

- With each inhalation, one experiences an increasing sense of relaxation.

- Inhale and exhale one last time, then proceed to close your eyes upon exhaling

- As you inhale and exhale, a growing lethargy weighs upon your eyes.

- While engaging in this meditation, focus your thoughts and adjust your posture, taking deep inhalations and exhalations to induce a state of body relaxation.

- You experience a growing sense of euphoria and deep relaxation setting in within your physical being.

- You perceive a sensation of your physical form gradually immersing into the mattress as you inhale and exhale.

- Permit your breath to operate in its inherent natural rhythm; simply allow your breathing to progress.

- Simply maintain your typical breathing rhythm and find solace in the calmness. Remind yourself, "

I possess an innate ability to indulge in profound and restful slumber.

- Ensure that you do not permit any distractions to hinder your ability to relax; remind yourself

I possess the ability to disengage from my thoughts.

- Inhale and exhale once more, experiencing increased relaxation

- Commence to value the tranquil environment that envelops you.

- Take heed of the soft resonance emanating from your breath, evoking an awareness of the profound depths of the ocean.

- Your breath is completely organic, and you appreciate the way it resembles the soothing sounds of the ocean.
- Inhale and exhale to induce a heightened state of relaxation and tranquility.
- As respiration progressively decelerates, one reaches a state of readiness to effortlessly transition into a serene and profound slumber.
- Your body finds pleasure in experiencing this new sensation of drifting into slumber.
- Allow your thoughts to transition towards your comfortable and inviting pillow.
- Experience and acknowledge the plushness and comfort of the pillow, enticing you to embrace a restful slumber.

Release tension from your physical being and recline upon this cushion.

- Inhale and exhale while experiencing a state of relaxation
- The auditory and cognitive aspects of this guide will gradually diminish,

allowing you to enter a state of repose on the wings of slumber.

- You shall experience a profound sense of relaxation and drowsiness, gradually descending into a heightened state of tranquility and sensory perception.

- Inhale and exhale deeply, allowing yourself to enter a state of deep and restful slumber.

- You are gradually experiencing a greater sense of relaxation and entering into a state akin to reverie.

- You appear to resemble an infant, peacefully slumbering and experiencing tranquil respiration.

- Inhale and exhale; you are cocooned in gentle coverings akin to a newborn.

- You are in a state of deep slumber, profoundly. You are deserving of a peaceful and rejuvenating slumber.

- Inhaling and exhaling without difficulty, and experiencing restful sleep, is inherent to your nature. Take deep breaths while you attain the necessary repose.

- And thus concludes the attainment of the restful sleep you have been diligently seeking.

Deep Sleep Facilitated by Abdominal Respiration

Throughout the day, as well as in the nighttime while reclined in your bed, adopting a practice of diaphragmatic breathing and redirecting your focus towards your breaths can facilitate a state of relaxation. Certain individuals prefer reclining in a room with subdued lighting, accompanied by gentle melodies, or gently shutting their eyes while directing their attention towards their breath.

As you recline in bed, endeavor to gently position your hands upon the abdominal region. Inhale and exhale slowly while delicately gliding your hands across the abdominal area. Directing your attention towards this motion diverts your mental energy away from distracting thoughts and redirects it towards the physique. It is an exceedingly tranquilizing activity that can facilitate restful slumber. Engage in this activity whilst in a reclining position before you intend to drift into slumber during the nocturnal hours and in instances where you awaken during the night and experience difficulty resuming slumber. It proves to be immensely advantageous when one's thoughts are preoccupied or racing, a phenomena frequently observed among individuals suffering from insomnia.

Assume a comfortable posture on your bed and allow yourself to unwind. Begin by attentively observing your physical state along with any other sensory perceptions that may arise. Attempt to become more attuned to the sensation of your body's physical contact with the surface upon which you are reclining, and consciously endeavor to release any tension that may be present. Additionally, consider the possibility of gently easing the tension within your muscles. Direct all of your concentration towards your physical being. However, in the event that your thoughts begin to drift, a phenomenon commonly observed during times of rest, endeavor to realign your focus towards your bodily sensations. Acquiring the skill to direct your attention solely towards your organization necessitates significant dedication and a prolonged period of practice.

Direct your attention towards your breathing, specifically the sensations you perceive in your body, most likely in your abdomen, and then concentrate on the entirety of each breath. Once more, in the event that your mind begins to stray, make an effort to redirect your focus towards your breath. Inhale deeply, directing your breath towards your lower abdomen and sense the expansion caused by the influx of air. Maintain the position momentarily, and subsequently release. Direct your attention to the gentle rise and fall of your abdomen, and consciously observe the inhalation and exhalation of the breath for several repetitions. Envision the process by which this air gradually occupies the abdominal cavity, subsequently traversing the respiratory passages in a repetitive pattern. Engage in this action in a repetitive manner while observing the areas of your physical being wherein tension is experienced. Proceed to alleviate said tension by consciously directing your breath towards the specific region.

Fundamental Sleep Meditation Template

There are a few factors that need to be considered with regards to achieving and maintaining a state of sleep.

If you belong to the majority, it is likely that your mind is occupied with various thoughts and concerns that prevent you from sleeping. Persistent mental agitation will impede your ability to enter a state of restful slumber. Although this guided meditation for sleep can offer some relief, it is imperative that you exert personal effort to achieve desired results. Similar to your ability to calm your mind in stressful situations, you will need to instruct your mind to quiet down when you are prepared to conclude your day.

My perpetual recommendation is to establish a regular schedule upon deciding to retire for the night. One practice that may prove helpful in calming your mind is to maintain a notebook on your bedside table. With this item within reach, you have the ability to record any pivotal ideas you wish to retain. In this manner, you are able to prompt yourself regarding any matter tomorrow. It is essential to remind oneself that such thoughts will only serve to disturb a serene and restful night's sleep. Please record your reflections and refrain from dwelling on them.

Once you assess that you are primed for sleep, make the necessary preparations to ensure a successful rest. Ensure that all necessary preparations for the following day are attended to, be it the preparation of your lunch or the selection of your attire. Please ensure that you engage in oral hygiene by brushing your teeth, change into your most comfortable sleepwear, proceed to turn off the lights, and carefully settle into bed.

If you feel at ease, I kindly extend an invitation for you to assume a prone position on your back. After discovering a suitable position, it is advisable to allow your legs and arms to assume a resting posture in the most comfortable manner. Should you experience any discomfort at any point during this meditation, please feel free to adjust and alter your position accordingly. Currently, I suggest assuming a supine position to enhance your comfort, and subsequently, we can commence.

Once you have taken your place and become comfortable, please proceed with initiating your body scan exercise. Please ensure that you refrain from passing judgment on any thoughts that may arise. Presently, our consciousness is solely gravitating towards our physical beings. Currently, there exists no exigency to make any alterations. Conduct a thorough examination for instances of muscular tension and redirect your attention towards relieving the regions that perceive heightened tightness. As one attains greater consciousness, one observes the gradual cultivation of tranquility within the mind. You are establishing a profound and exquisite linkage between the faculties of the mind and the physical dimensions of the body. You possess the ability to govern your thoughts, allowing you to calm your mind and attain adequate rest for the forthcoming day.

When you are ready, take a sweet deep breath in. Permit the inhalation of air to infuse you with vitality and surrender yourself to the growing tranquility that is enveloping your being. Breathe out, release any tension that you have observed. While you persist in engaging in the act of respiration, it is likely that reflections pertaining to the current day shall inundate your cognitive faculties. It is possible that your mind is also being obscured by thoughts regarding the tasks that you have to accomplish tomorrow. In the event that there are any matters of utmost importance, please ensure they are recorded in writing. These thoughts hold no significance for you at present.

When one exhibits conscious awareness of the present moment, the significance of the preceding and subsequent periods becomes superfluous. Currently, you are in the process of attaining a state of tranquility, and eagerly anticipaing a pleasant period of relaxation.

Encourage the passage of all thoughts devoid of subjective evaluation. Your current priority should be directing your attention towards the sensations in your body. Inhale and exhale. Encourage the departure of all thoughts from your mind. For the ensuing moments, I kindly request that you commence enumerating every inhalation and exhalation. Delicately tally each breath in and perceive the growing sense of relaxation with each consecutive numeral. Enumerate from one to ten while progressively succumbing to a heightened state of relaxation within the confines of your resting place.

Direct your attention to the number one in a gentle manner... Inhale deeply and release all tension.

Two...perceive the dissipation of tension throughout your entire physique. Your bed is so comfortable and warm and inviting you to fall asleep safely.

Three...you are experiencing an increasing sense of relaxation. You eagerly anticipate a restful slumber, which will greatly contribute to your preparedness for a successful day ahead.

Your cognitive faculties are becoming remarkably tranquil, as evidenced by the number four. Your mind is occupied solely by pleasant dreams.

Five...you are drifting now. Notice the weight of your body as it rests upon the bed. Your cognitive faculties are prepared to cease their activities momentarily. Your physique is prepared to engage in a period of rest and recuperation.

Six...you are feeling wonderful and safe. You are at ease and gradually entering a state of relaxation...

Seven...so calm. So happy. So relaxed.

Eight...heavy. Calm. Relaxed.

Nine...take gentle breaths, allowing yourself to become prepared to peacefully transition and enter into a state of slumber...

Ten...

If you are still marginally alert, please persist in tallying each inhalation and exhalation. Take notice of the significant weight that your eyelids are carrying. Your physical state is characterized by warmth and security as you lay in the confines of your bed. You are drifting...

Drifting...

Drifting...

Sleep...

The enduring consequences of stress on professional and personal associations.

In addition to the impact on your well-being, stress can have detrimental consequences on both your personal and professional spheres. Let us examine the hazards that are associated with this situation.

You are susceptible to experiencing burnout. The ultimate undesirable scenario entails experiencing work-related burnout. That is highly likely to result in a significant decline in your productivity. Moreover, it should be noted that engaging in such frenzied work habits not only increases the risk of burnout but also severely hampers productivity, falling far below the desired level. Moreover, one finds oneself awaking each morning with the notion that going to work has become a daily obligation. By the conclusion of the day, you experience an overwhelming sense of fatigue, accompanied by a profound realization that you possess no semblance of authority over the unfolding events that potentially encompass your life. You may even find yourself desiring a replica of yourself to collaborate with in order to ensure timely completion of the tasks at hand. Overall, it appears that you do not derive satisfaction from your job and instead carry out your tasks mechanically, devoid of enthusiasm.

Your interpersonal connections with both friends and family are adversely impacted. Due to excessive workload, there is an inevitable significant deterioration in your relationships with your loved ones. You have become increasingly unenjoyable to be around, and it is possible that you may experience more individuals distancing themselves from you than you would from them. You experience a state of irritability and displeasure, leading to a preference for seclusion within your room rather than attending social gatherings characterized by exuberance and merriment, which are seemingly incompatible with your current emotional state. This type of disproportion between work and personal life eliminates any available time for significant moments in life, such as attending your son's baseball game or your daughter's ballet concert. This can incite an elevation in your temper, resulting in internalized anger that will subsequently impact the quality of your work.

There is a possibility that you may be at risk of losing your employment or failing to secure that advancement opportunity. These perilous levels of stress can have an adverse impact on your work, potentially jeopardizing your chances of securing the long-desired promotion and even, ultimately, putting your job at risk. This has the potential to completely upend your entire life, and not only will it be too late to rectify the present situation, but it can also exacerbate your mental state. Indeed, it could have been effectively managed and addressed much earlier.

The Importance of Brief Meditation Sessions

At this point, it is likely that you have comprehended the growing necessity for you to allocate a mere five minutes of your time for brief meditation exercises. Let us explore the advantages that can be derived from engaging in these brief mindfulness exercises.

They are considerably more manageable to accomplish. It is a fact that you will achieve a significantly higher level of effectiveness in practicing those five-minute meditations compared to engaging in longer meditation sessions. The answer is quite evident: you do not necessitate the level of concentration that longer durations of meditation entail. Moreover, due to their brevity, one can potentially engage in these activities multiple times within a given day to enhance their efficacy.

Physical benefits. You will receive the full range of physiological advantages associated with extended periods of meditation, such as optimized blood pressure, enhanced immune system functionality, and a noticeable elevation in overall vitality.

Mental benefits. The cognitive advantages derived from the practice of meditation are indeed substantial. You shall observe a significant reduction in the levels of anxiety and depression, accompanied by an enhanced sense of tranquility and mental lucidity. Your challenges will gradually diminish in significance and subsequently contribute to a heightened sense of contentment. Consequently, it becomes even more imperative to initiate the incorporation of concise contemplative practices that will unequivocally enhance the caliber of the lifestyle you are currently leading.

A Brief Five-Minute Meditation For Relaxation Post-Work

Initial Step: Position oneself beneath the shower. Please take note of the auditory experience created by the flowing water contacting your body and the contrasting sound produced when you move away to apply soap, observing the sound of the water striking the floor.

Step Two: Consciously experience the sensation of water flowing over your body and meticulously attend to the sensations that accompany the application of soap and shampoo to cleanse your body. It is advisable to close your eyes when experiencing these pleasurable sensations.

Step Three: Envision the complete alleviation of stress as the water gently flows across your physique, purging it from any accumulated impurities that may have gathered throughout the preceding hours. Consider all the elements to which you are emotionally attached - your aspirations and personal connections. Consider the notion of their eradication, and you will discover an emancipation from all the constraints that tether you. You are solely giving your attention to the auditory perception of the water as it flows over your physical form and the accompanying sonic emissions it generates while doing so.

Step Four: Visualize the descending water as a manifestation of immaculate luminosity. Ensure that you possess unwavering faith in the efficacy of this luminous entity to provide adequate protection, while acknowledging that there exists no legitimate cause for trepidation in the external realm. Imagine this luminous aura enveloping you like a protective shield.

Step Five: Once you exit the shower, take a moment to experience the soothing feeling that comes from the touch of the towel as you gently pat and dry your skin. Observe the remarkable sensation that this evokes within you. Please be aware that this is a potential option that can be pursued for various reasons, such as prior to a board meeting, in the event that there is a shower available at the office facility. If you are disinclined to shower at the workplace, opting for music instead would be a viable alternative, and the advantage of making this choice would solely be your own. Discover the optimal approach for oneself and diligently adhere to it in order to attain the most favorable desired outcomes.

Regularly attending the gym is of utmost importance, while ensuring to engage in meditation prior to a workout holds equal significance in order to derive the utmost advantages from these activities. Let us examine how we can achieve the same outcome.

A Brief Meditation Session Prior to Commencing Physical Exercise

Firstly, engage in diaphragmatic breathing. You are advised to recline in a supine position during this form of meditation and intentionally amplify the inward motion of the abdomen while inhaling. Likewise, it is imperative that during exhalation, a significant outward movement of the abdomen is exhibited.

Continue doing this until you have attained a state of adequate relaxation.

Secondly, engage in mental imagery to vividly envision the specific physique you aspire to attain, embracing the complete transformation once your desired physical appearance has been fully achieved. This practice will have a soothing effect on your mind by encouraging the visualization of positive images, thereby enhancing your ability to carry out the exercise with increased enthusiasm.

Upon the completion of your workout session, when you find yourself seated for a meal, you may perhaps consider allocating an additional five minutes for the purpose of engaging in meditation immediately thereafter. Please consider partaking in a brief, yet powerful, five-minute meditation routine prior to your evening meal.

A Brief Pre-Dinner Meditation Exercise

First Step: Gently close your eyes while seated at the dining table and consciously cultivate a profound sense of appreciation for the abundance of nourishment that is before you.

Secondly, following the cultivation of gratitude, it is advisable to engage in a series of deep breaths prior to commencing the act of consuming food. Direct your attention solely to your breath and exclude all other thoughts and distractions. Merely observe the inhalation and exhalation of your breath. Ensure that you redirect your attention to your breathing, even though thoughts of food and other distractions may arise in your mind. This will guarantee that you cultivate a heightened sense of awareness during the act of eating in the future, enabling you to be fully present in the current moment. Attaining this state of mindfulness aligns with the core objective of every meditative practice.

Ultimately, it is imperative that we all engage in the act of sleeping, as the caliber of our sleep significantly influences the outcome of the following day. Indeed, there is ample evidence to support the notion that individuals who consistently obtain a restful night's sleep are the individuals who excel in their professional endeavors. Upon integrating this efficient and uncomplicated five-minute meditation into your routine, it will become evident that the caliber of your sleep will experience a significant enhancement over an extended duration, allowing you to approach the forthcoming day equipped with a revitalized determination. Now, let us proceed to examine it likewise.

A brief five-minute meditation to practice prior to your slumber

First step: Ensure that you power down all electronic devices at least one hour prior to your intended bedtime. This can be attributed to the fact that the 'blue light' emitted by these devices acts as a stimulant for the mind, preventing it from achieving the necessary level of relaxation required for a meditation intended to enhance sleep quality.

Second Step: One should engage in abdominal breathing without assuming a supine position, as recommended in the previously mentioned pre-gym meditation. Ensure that you maintain an erect posture while engaging in meditation on your bed.

Proceed to the third step by positioning your hands upon your abdomen, enabling them to move gracefully in sync with the inhalation and exhalation of your breath. This allows you to focus on your body and thus helps to calm that thought process that is responsible for thoughts coursing senselessly through your mind all the time.

Step Four: Employ the technique of 'Guided Imagery'. It is highly advisable to strive for a state of utmost tranquility at the conclusion of each day. To achieve this, one way that proves exceptionally effective is to envision a serene landscape such as majestic mountains, ethereal clouds, or the vast expanse of the ocean. With the power of imagination, one has the ability to envision an inviting realm, engaging all senses in the process of exploration. Remarkably, our minds often fail to distinguish between reality and the realm of imagination. Thus, one may find solace and tranquility by immersing oneself in breathtaking landscapes, transcending the boundaries of the tangible world.

Step Five: Let go. Once the guided imagery process comes to an end, select a prevailing issue in your life that appears to overpower your thoughts and release it, allowing it to no longer have a hold on you. By adopting this approach, you will not only guarantee an enhanced quality of sleep but also witness a diminishment in the aforementioned problem. Undoubtedly a mutually beneficial scenario arises when considering the utilization of this brief five-minute meditation prior to your slumber.

www.ingramcontent.com/pod-product-compliance
Lightning Source LLC
Chambersburg PA
CBHW050253120526
44590CB00016B/2331